Desert Critter Friends

Friendly Differences

Mona Gansberg Hodgson
Illustrated by Chris Sharp

SAINT LOUIS

*Dedicated in fond memory to my father,
William Bert Gansberg, who loved children,
the desert, and God.*

*Special thanks to Susan Titus Osborn, Nancy
Sanders, and Christine Tangvald for using
their gifts to write children's books and to
help teach me to do the same.*

Desert Critter Friends Series

Friendly Differences

Thorny Treasures

Sour Snacks

Smelly Tales

Clubhouse Surprises

Desert Detectives

Scripture quotations taken from the HOLY BIBLE, NEW INTERNATIONAL VERSION®. NIV®. Copyright © 1973, 1978, 1984 by International Bible Society. Used by permission of Zondervan Publishing House. All rights reserved.
Copyright © 1998 Mona Gansberg Hodgson
Published by Concordia Publishing House
3558 S. Jefferson Avenue, St. Louis, MO 63118-3968
Manufactured in the United States of America

Library of Congress Cataloging-in-Publication Data
Hodgson, Mona Gansberg, 1954–
    Friendly differences / Mona Gansberg Hodgson.
        p.   cm. — (Desert critter friends series ; bk 1)
    Summary: Bert the roadrunner and Taylor the tortoise come to the conclusion that, despite their differences, God had a reason for making them the way they are, and they can still be friends.
    Includes a Bible verse and activities.
        [1. Roadrunner—Fiction. 2. Turtles—Fiction. 3. Deserts—Fiction. 4. Individuality—Fiction. 5. Christian life—Fiction.]
    I. Title. II. Series: Desert critter friends ; bk. 1.
PZ7.H6649Fr   1998
[E]—dc21
                                                                97-25831

2 3 4 5 6 7 8 9 10 11   08 07 06 05 04 03 02 01 00 99

Bert, the roadrunner, set
breakfast down on his table. Then
he poured two glasses of cactus
juice.

Just then Bert's neighbor Myra
came to the door. "Hello in there!"
the quail said.

Bert poked his fuzzy head out
of his mesquite bush house. "Good
morning, Myra," he said. He looked
up at the rising sun. "You're right
on time. Come in. Come in."

The two friends sat down across from each other.

"Have-some-cactus-juice,-Myra,-it's-good-for-you," Bert said. It sounded like just one word.

Myra giggled. "You do everything fast," she said. "You even talk fast!"

"That's just the way I am." Bert grabbed a cactus apple and began munching. Myra sipped her juice.

Myra pushed her glasses closer to her face. "*Hmmm.* It looks like you could use some help cleaning up this place," she said.

"Not today," Bert said. "I have big plans!" He gobbled his last bite of cactus apple. Then he jumped up and pulled his backpack off a branch.

"I'm going to explore the
desert! Want to come?" Bert asked.
He packed stuff in his backpack. In
went a flashlight. Then a water
bottle. Then some snacks. Bert
studied his map for a minute.
"Today's my day to explore all the
way to the bottom of Mingus
Mountain."

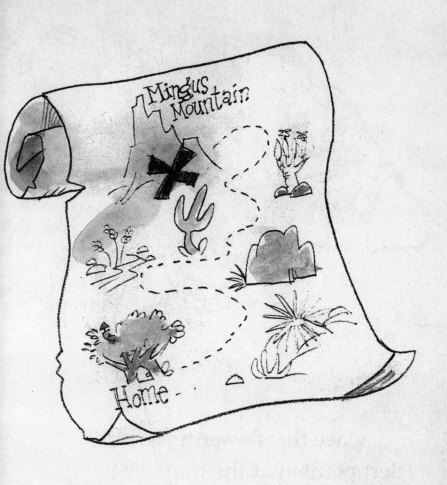

Myra looked at Bert's map. "It looks like you plan to be gone all day."

"You bet! Want to come?"

"See this flowering cactus?"
Bert pointed at the map. "We'll go
past it. Then we'll go over these big
rocks and around this bunch of
trees. It takes all day to get to
Mingus Mountain and back."

"I'll go part way," Myra said.
"Then I'll need to come home.

Fergus, the owl, is coming over for lunch." Myra brushed the crumbs off the table.

"Let's go!" Bert yanked his cap off a twig. He darted out of his bush house. Myra scurried out behind him.

SCREECHH...

The spicy smell of the yellow sage bushes tickled Bert's nose. Bert's toes stretched down into the warm sand. *Squish! Squish!*

Zoom! Bert took off. He ran so fast that dirt flew out behind him. Myra hurried over an ant hill.

Zoom! Bert ran through a valley.

"Hey! Wait for me," Myra shouted.

Screech! Bert put on his brakes. "Come on!" he called, waiting for Myra to catch up.

15

Bert zoomed around three bushes. Myra ducked under three branches.

Bert zipped over two rocks. Myra ran around a flowering cactus. "I'm thirsty," she panted.

Bert stopped. Myra took three sips from Bert's water bottle. Bert took a huge gulp of water.

"It's time for me to go back home," Myra said. She started walking toward home. "Good-bye, Bert. See you tomorrow at breakfast."

"Good-bye," said Bert. Then he turned and jumped over some rocks. He raced through a valley and over a hill. *Zoom!*

"Ouch!" a voice said.

Screech! Bert stopped running. He looked left. He looked right. Where had the voice come from?

"Who's there?" Bert asked. He tipped his fuzzy head.

"I'm Taylor," said the voice. "Don't step on me again. And don't kick sand in my face."

"I stepped on someone?" Bert asked. Again he looked left. Again he looked right. Where had the voice come from?

Bert didn't see a face in the bushes. He didn't see a face behind the log. He didn't see a face in the rocks.

"Where are you?" Bert shouted.

"Down here," the voice said, "under my shell."

Bert looked down on the ground. He was standing in front of a strange-looking rock. Bert pulled his map out of his backpack. This rock wasn't on his map. He jammed the map back into his backpack.

The rock crept forward! Bert saw a book on the ground where the rock had been.

"Is that you? Are you a moving rock? Why do you sit on a book?" Bert asked.

"I rest on my book," Taylor said. "And please don't step on me again."

"Well, I'll try not to," Bert said. *"Where is your face?"*

"If you promise to stand still," Taylor said, "I will show you my face."

Bert hopped on a log. "I will stand still, very still."

Pop! A bald brown head poked out of the rock.

Bert didn't stand still. He flapped his wings. He fell off the log.

Taylor pulled his head back into his shell. His shell went up and down. Up and down. Up and down.

Bert got back on his feet. His mouth dropped open. "Why are you doing push-ups?"

"I do this when I'm nervous. I'm nervous because you didn't stand still!"

"Sorry! But what kind of an animal are you?"

"I'm a tortoise. Like a turtle, only different. Haven't you ever seen a tortoise or a turtle?"

"A tortoise? I've never seen anyone like you before." Bert crept closer to Taylor. A tortoise was something new to explore. "Do you live here?"

"Only in the summer," answered Taylor. "When it gets cold, I go back to the lower desert. It's warmer there."

Bert lowered his head and stared at Taylor. "That's your face?"

"Yes. This is my face!" The tortoise eased his head back out of the shell.

"Where's your fuzz?" Bert giggled. He walked around the tortoise. "Where are your feathers? And your legs—well—they are short!"

"This is the face God gave me," Taylor said. "And these are the legs God gave me! What's wrong with them?"

"*Gulp.* Nothing," Bert said. He took off his cap. "It's just that—well—you look different!"

"You're the one who looks funny," Taylor said. He raised up on his legs and walked around Bert. "Your head is frizzy like a bush. Your legs are skinny like twigs. Your toes look like nails. And you look like you have a fan sticking out of your backside."

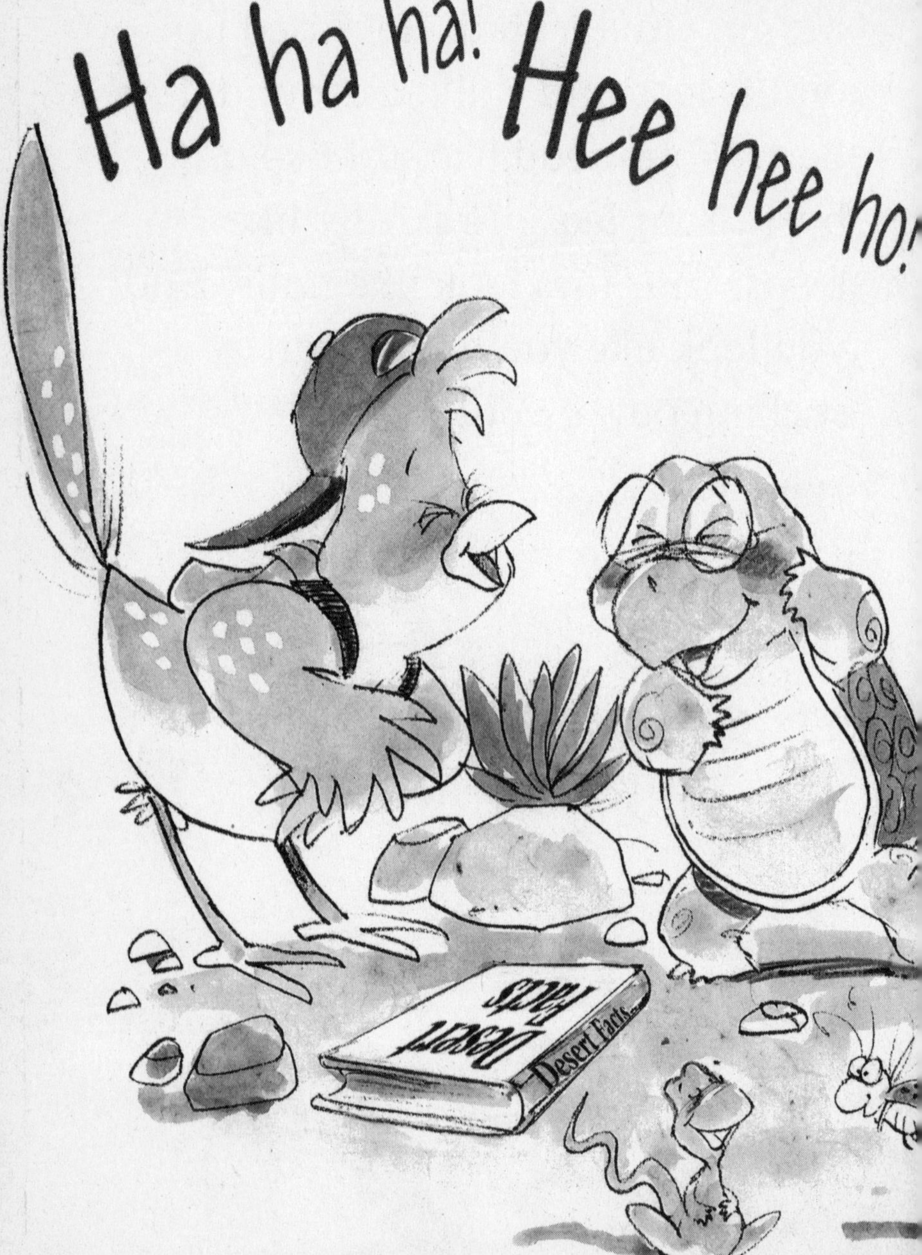

"Ha! Ha! Ha!" Bert laughed.

"Hee! Hee! Ho!" Taylor laughed too.

"I never thought about it that way," Bert said. "I guess we're both different." He put his cap back on his head. "Do you want to come explore with me?"

"No thanks," Taylor answered. "You are too fast for me. You zoom and I creep. I'll just sit and read my book for a while."

Bert looked at Taylor's book. It was called *Desert Facts*. "I guess you are right," Bert said. "We are too different." He zoomed away.

Bert raced through the desert. He hurried over big rocks. His feet made a cloud of dust behind him. He could see a clump of trees. He was getting close to the bottom of Mingus Mountain. Then he saw something shiny.

Screech! Bert stopped and bent down for a better look. It was a can. He picked it up and put it in his backpack. He grabbed a couple of mesquite seedpods from his backpack and munched them.

Zoom! Bert took off again.

Bert hopped around small rocks. He ducked under a branch. He zipped around a clump of cottonwood trees. He stopped in a dry gully. He rubbed his neck on a piece of smooth wood. Then he put the wood in his backpack and took off again. He was almost to Mingus Mountain.

Whew! He had made it. He had explored all the way to the bottom of Mingus Mountain.

Bert looked up at the mountain. The sun was setting. He decided he should head for home.

Bert darted around a clump of trees. He stopped in the dry gully. Bert guzzled from his water bottle. Then he spotted some tiny shiny things in the dirt. He had never seen anything like them. They were a mystery.

Bert studied them. What were they? They looked kind of like polished rocks. He turned one over with his spiked toe. It was white and open on one end. He wished he knew what they were. He put three of them in his backpack. How could he find out what they were?

Bert hurried over big rocks. He raced through the desert. Suddenly Bert tumbled over Taylor!

Bert's backpack flew through the air. The flashlight dropped out. The water bottle crashed to the ground. The map fell to the dirt. The mystery stones tumbled out.

"Oh, wow!" Taylor shouted.
"You have some!"

"I have bumps on my head.
That's what I have." Bert rubbed
his head with his wing. "You
stepped out right in front of me."

39

Bert tugged the backpack off a bush with his beak.

"Sorry about that, but I must see these," Taylor said. He looked at Bert's mystery stones. "You explored the riverbed!"

"I stopped in a dry gully," Bert answered.

"That's it!" Taylor said. "When

the Verde River changes its path, it makes dry gullies where the water used to flow. I was just reading about it in my book."

Bert pointed to the mystery stones. "Do you know what these are?"

"Sure. They are in my book too." Taylor tucked in his front legs. His book slid off of his back and over his head.

"Really?" Bert bent down to look in Taylor's book.

Taylor pointed to a page with his foot. "Right here. See. They are called freshwater clamshells."

"I'm glad that you know all this stuff," Bert said.

"I like to read," Taylor said. "I think it's great that you can run and find all this stuff." He looked at the clamshells. "Maybe we're *not* too different to be friends."

Bert nodded his fuzzy head. "I'm glad we're friends," he said. He started flipping the book's pages. "What do you want me to find for you the next time I go exploring?"

God made you to be you. He made your friends to be like themselves. He loves you all so much that He sent His Son to die for you. Celebrate your friendly differences.

I praise you because I am fearfully and wonderfully made. Psalm 139:14

The word search on the next page is full of the animals, birds, plants, and places you read about in this story. See if you can find them all.

cactus

clamshell

desert

gully

mesquite

owl

quail

roadrunner

sage

tortoise

M	O	D	E	S	E	R	T	E	R
E	C	W	G	T	L	Q	G	E	C
S	P	L	L	R	L	A	N	Y	A
Q	Q	D	A	R	S	N	J	L	C
U	U	J	Q	M	U	R	Z	E	T
I	A	E	C	R	S	L	Z	D	U
T	I	M	D	L	X	H	H	U	S
E	L	A	Q	G	F	A	E	E	T
Q	O	Q	G	U	L	L	Y	L	S
R	T	O	R	T	O	I	S	E	L

For Parents and Teachers:

Physical and mental differences can make us self-conscious and uncomfortable. If we're honest we have to admit that at one time or another, like Bert and Taylor, we have been surprised, annoyed, or even embarrassed by someone else's physical differences. Furthermore, most of us (kids and adults) struggle to accept our own differences.

We all take comfort in the truth that God created us and loves us as we are. He didn't make us on an assembly line so we'd all be the same. He created us as individuals with a special purpose.

Help your children to see that they are carefully and wonderfully made by God. Celebrate the unique qualities with which God has gifted you and your children. Praise Him for loving you enough to have sent His own Son to be your Savior from sin and death.

Here are some questions you can use as discussion starters to help your children understand these concepts.

Discussion Starters

1. Where does Bert, the roadrunner, live?

2. What other animals and plants were mentioned in the story?

3. What other animals and insects might you see in the desert?

4. Why did Bert and Taylor laugh at each other?

5. How were Bert and Taylor different from each other?

6. How are you different from other kids?

7. Read Psalm 139:13–14 together. What do these words say about the way God made us?

8. Bert and Taylor became friends, even though they looked very different from each other. Are there some people you could become friends with, even if they are different from you?

Pray together. Thank God for sending His Son to be your Savior. Ask God to help you look for things you have in common with someone who seems different from you.